A Flash of Lightning

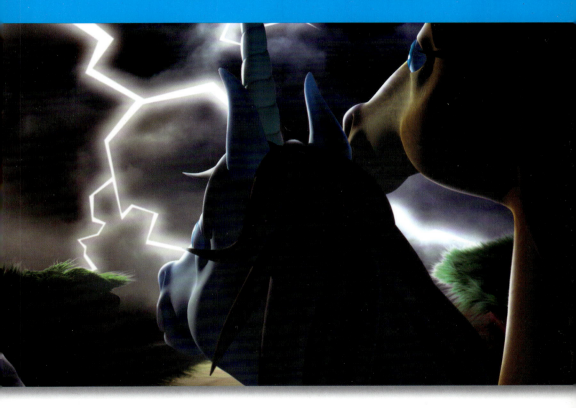

Written by Lisa Thompson
Pictures by Luke Jurevicius, Toby Quarmby and Arthur Moody

Flash!

There was a big flash of lightning. It lit up the sky.

FLASH!

Big Eyes looked up.

"A big storm is coming," he said. "I will stay here, in my tree."

"I don't like lightning," said Binks.

She hid in her bed.

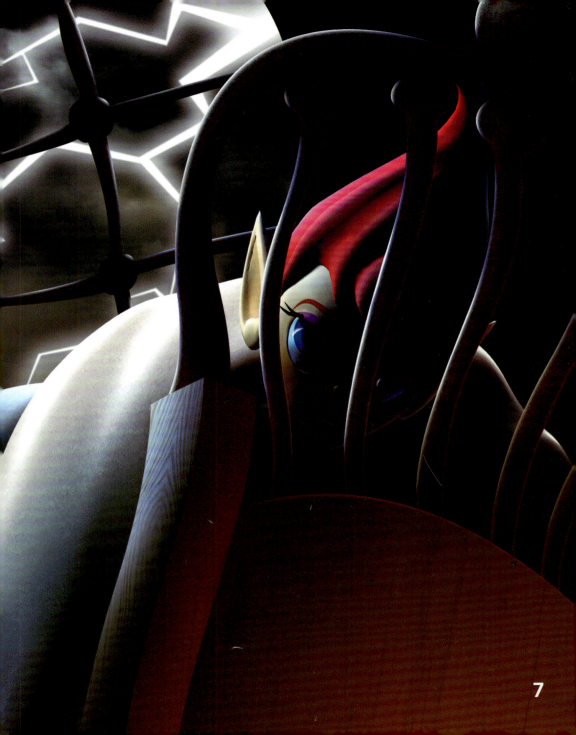

"Oh no!" said Hector. "Not a storm! I don't like it. I don't like it at all."

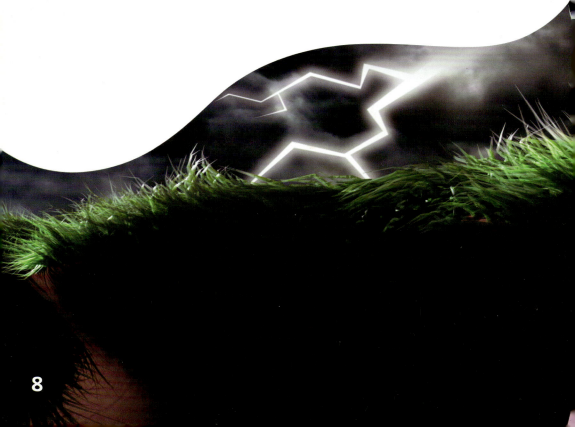

Boo looked at the lightning.

"I don't like lightning," he said. "I like to stay in the dark."

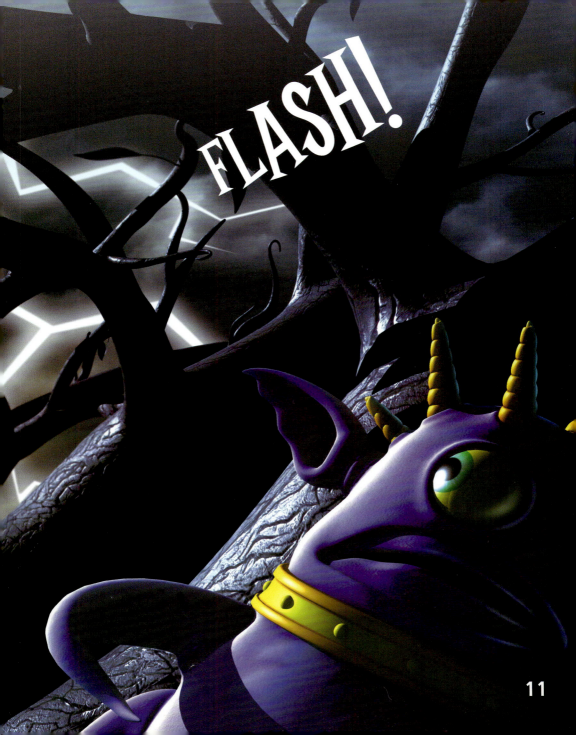

"Oh no!" said Dash. "The rain is coming."

She hid in the cave with her friend.

"I **like** storms!" said Gog. "I like looking at the lightning, and I like staying here, in bed!"

Match Me!

"A big storm is coming,"

... said Gog the giant.

"Oh no! Not a storm!"

... said Big Eyes the owl.

"I **like** storms!"

... said Hector the troll.